The Cryptic Mind and the Deciphered Heart

Luke Harvey

BookLeaf Publishing
India | USA | UK

The Cryptic Mind and the Deciphered Heart

Presentation by *BookLeaf Publishing*

Web: www.bookleafpub.com

E-mail: info@bookleafpub.com

ISBN : 9789357442176

First edition 2023

Hope

When you feel your hope is gone, know that it is not lost, but that it is only on a journey - it will return. And when it returns, it will be strengthened and renewed. But it will not return alone. No, it will be accompanied by faith. Faith is the backbone on which hope supports itself. Together, this combination transforms into the strongest weapon man can possess and cannot be stripped away. Not only is it the strongest weapon, but the most dangerous as well. It is the most feared amongst your enemies whether it is admitted or not.

Faith supercharges hope and launches it to a higher plane, strengthening it to take on the impossible.
Hope gives a man a reason to get back up, a reason to stand, a reason to fight for what he believes in. Hope gives a man purpose, to do what is right, to never back down no matter the cost. Hope gives a man belief – the belief that there is still a chance to take a stand, to make a statement, to make a change.

September 20, 2013

In the Blink of an Eye

Life. One day you're in a field of flowers,
the next you're in a fight for the ages.
One swing comes after another
and you feel locked inside a cage.
Upside down and inside out,
not knowing which way is up;
You think you have your center, but realize it's
not enough.

Life hits hard and it will leave
you beaten and emotionally bruised.
Mentally the hits will take their toll,
leaving you lost and confused.
Laughter will ease the pain
while tears make it all real;
But it's the special ones with you along the path
who will help you heal.

Now there is going to come a time
where you're teetering on the brink;
And the world changes in front of you
faster than you can blink.
Standing on that edge
you're ready to make your move;
Only to encounter there's a fork
in the middle of your route.
That fork may be now,
it's passed, or it's near;
But one thing's for certain,
that fork will always appear.

So hold on to your faith and stand your ground,
trust in who you are.
Listen to your gut and don’t be moved
as life tries to rip you apart.
You are stronger than you think
and may not realize it yet;
But you have a battalion by your side,
to your front, and to your back.
So don’t be afraid by that unknown
fork in life’s winding road.
Just remember you are not alone to carry that
heavy load.

January 6, 2023

The Overthinker

Overthinking is an art. It isn't for the
weak-minded.
One minute you're confident, the next you're
blind-sided.

Your mind kicks into overdrive second guessing
everything;
Reliving each word and action – damn, the mind
is unyielding.

It isn't a matter of confidence – there's plenty to
go around.
No, it's a matter of perfection, ensuring
everything is sound.

Before thoughts become action every scenario is
played out
In the mind as each little detail whirls about.

And once the bell has been rung and thought
comes to fruition,
Regret seeps in…questioning intuition.

Overcome the mind, it's time to face the truth;
Stop questioning oneself and get back to the
roots.

Water those roots with overwhelming tears,
May they wash away all of the unfounded fears.

Stand by the words that have been said and
deeds that have been done;
Fight or flight shouldn't always be option
number one.

Find what brings joy and inspires peace;
Allowing to live only in the moment and to not
overthink.

January 22, 2023

Night's Light

When the nights are dark and full of torment
And you're tired of counting sheep.
When the carousel of thoughts keeps going
And you cry yourself to sleep.

Just remember that even angels cry
And the day is racing to you;
With the sun to dry away your tears,
Your hero to the rescue.

But should night's darkness shroud your light
And loneliness break your spirit;
Just tilt your head to the moon above
For the sun is reflecting in it.

The stars will guide you through the night,
The moon will light your way.
Until you've reached the journey's end
And you are happy once again.

January 8, 2023

A Reintroduction

So much time has passed, I've forgotten where
I've been;
The more I look around, the more I have to look
within.

The fate of tomorrow is teed up by what happens
today;
To learn the day's lesson, sometimes you have to
hit replay.

Falling into the past with old poems and old
writings;
Breaking open old journals and cracking brittle
bindings.

With wine in hand, brought to lips, solitude by
fire's light,
I dig deep within, searching, as I begin to write...

Hello to self, it's been a while, since we last met;
Reintroducing pen to paper and the ink is still
wet.

Looking back as I reflect - Where have you
gone, where am I going?
You have been adjacent while I climb out of
mind's purgatory.

But have faith in me and have faith in thyself;
I'm stepping out strong and making my presence
felt!

Reigniting, rekindling, stoking my fire through
my writing;
To get in sync while readjusting, reshaping, and
realigning.

February 12, 2018

A Lovely Thought

A quiet rage simmers to a boil
In the wake of unspeakable action.
Evil demonstrated in pure form
Has set the stage for reaction.

A reaction controlled by a narrative,
Like a hammer that drives a wedge.
A wedge creating chasmic division;
Division the agenda – unity left for dead.

But this agenda is already written,
Secretly added to the schedule.
The writing, though, is not our own,
But written by the hand of evil.

The agenda on the docket is to produce hate and villainize,
For friends to disagree.
We may not always see eye to eye;
That doesn't make us enemies.

Where is the unity among the tragedy?
Why do we persecute thoughts of others?
Treating our neighbor as our enemy,
Rather than our sister and brother.

We live in a time where thought is banned;
Where there's only one way to think.
Where good is bad and bad is good;
Revelations is starting to peak.

How do we fight back? What do we do?
We've given our thoughts and prayers.
It's time we love our neighbors as ourselves;
Even our enemies…if we dare.

May 22, 2022

Hero

Sometimes the hero in our lives is not who you'd expect…

Whoever they might be, keep in mind that maybe when they reach you they are battered and worn from the fight of trying to get to you. Their armor has gone from shiny and new to marred and tarnished; imperfect as the scars they wear are deep. They have been worn down, but have not faltered or swayed – they have dug in deep and held on through the storms. They have been beaten down, nearly broken throughout the journey, yet after each devastating blow have gotten back up to carry on, to find you, to reach you, and to save you.

Sometimes the hero in our lives is not who you'd expect…maybe your hero is not an outside source at all as maybe, just maybe, you are your own hero.

January 24, 2014

Re-Inspired

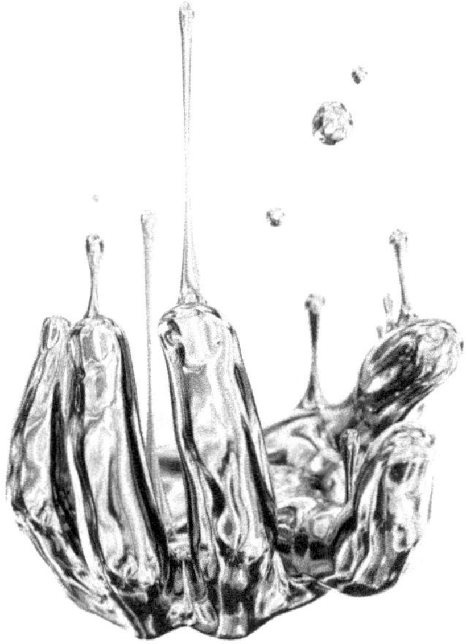

Re-inspired because I'm awe-inspired,
Let our words ring truth.
Pure, honest, unforced, untired,
Forever we'll be moved.

Not knowing what life supplies,
Or blessing 'round the bend.
May every day be a surprise,
And treasure it in your hand.

Don't take off your cross for anyone,
Leave it on for all to see.
May it remind them of where you're from
And reflect your honesty.

I continue to live by who I am
With intense integrity.
You ask why I'm a gentleman,
I guess it just comes naturally.

This is it, my confession of truth,
Long-live this glorious day.
I now hold out my hand to you,
Together, let's be on our way.

May 22, 2013

Stained Glass

Chaotic perfection framed in harmony,
Transformed light piercing through;
Broken colors caught in space
Shining cathartic hues.

Gripping darkness like the dawning sun,
Casting light upon shadows within;
Warm peace of color surrounds,
Gently kissing across your skin.

I am but stained glass,
Bringing light through imperfection;
Frail as silence yet resilient as love,
Complete through connection.

The myriad pieces of my life
Forged together through love and pain;
Only then can my colors be seen
As light shines through my pane.

November 12, 2021

The Battle of the Mind

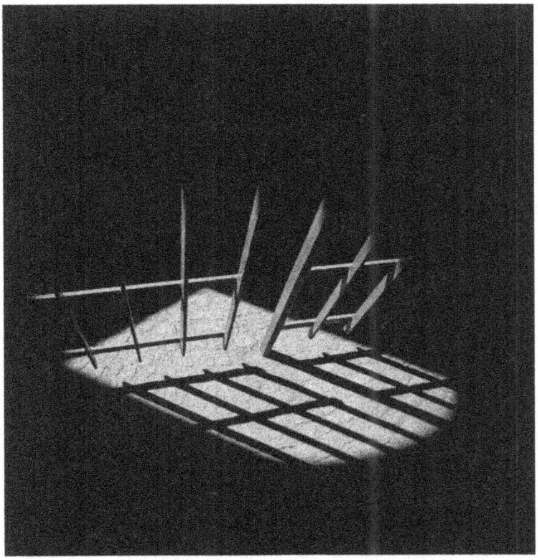

The mind can be a most dangerous place - weaving a web of self-deceit, what-ifs, and what-nots. Intricately spiraling lies out of truths, imagination from reality, and scenarios out of nothingness. Voicing what it wants to hear while starving itself of what it should say. It becomes caught in this tangled web of shattered dreams, just to discover a dysfunctional hope. Ironically, the only thing that can save the mind from the mind is the mind itself.
It is both the villain and the hero, fighting in a tumultuous battle of sanity.

January 21, 2014

The Ace

Forsaken or not, I will always be true;
God, give me strength as I listen to you.

My life right now is a quandary – convoluted at best;
I can't sit still much longer, but I need some damn rest.

Forgotten, but forgiven, what happens to me now?
The jury's still out as judgment hangs in the clouds.

Mistake this not as an attempted sadden decree;
This is rather a small way into understanding some of me.

So why do I sometimes write better than I speak?
So my voice can be read again, unlike verbal speech.

Life is best lived without guilt and regret,
And jealousy, fear, or shallow in depth.

I divulge myself and become vulnerable almost to fault;
I do not hide who I am or keep it locked in a vault.

I am one of a kind, the rarest of all makes…
The best card in your hand, I'm the illustrious ace of spades.

May 5, 2013

The Essence Of...

Dancing in the dark of night,
The way you sway from side to side,
Seduces the moon to shine its light;
Worthy only to reflect in your eyes.

Captivating eyes filled with fire and passion;
It's enough to bring me to my knees.
Captured by your look, you have my attention;
Never turning away from your beauty I see.

The authentic, all-encompassing beauty you
possess,
Brings a shivering warmth deep to my core.
Inward and Outward beauty entwined connect,
Radiating through that smile of yours.

Your smile, oh God your ever-infectious smile,
Injects me with your undiluted happiness;
Greeting me, healing me, from across the tiles,
All the while prescribing it with your lips.

Enchanted lips of an angel, lead to sing,
Guiding me to the voice of a goddess.
Gentle in tone with a strong undertow when sung,
I hypnotizingly delight in your sound of bliss.

August 21, 2013

I've Forgotten How To Play

Watching my son I think back and reflect
While he laughs and learns I strive to connect.
Drifting back to times of younger days,
Realizing that I've forgotten how to play.

I miss what it meant to be carefree;
To let loose my soul and to just be.
I miss the moments that lasted for days;
Dancing in the sun, resting in the shade.

My present desperately trying to cling to my past
Just like my son reaching up for his Dad.
Reflecting love and laughter through everyday
He brings me youth and teaches me how to play.

Gleaning this is a two-way street
That there is a time to learn and a time to teach.
Teaching my son to be a gentleman
While learning to be his age once again.

One day those small steps will take large strides,
Taking him along the path of life.
Don't take for granted these simple days
And never forget again how to play.

October 9, 2021

The Hopeful Romantic

Verily, I say unto you…
Romance is not dead, it is only for the strong at heart;
If you aren't ready for it, it will only tear you apart.
It will leave you beaten and confused, tattered and abused;
You'll be looking around, stunned, and wondering what just happened to you.

But if you are ready for it, you will be blessed far beyond your years,
Because it will kindle your passion of yearning for her and strike away any fear.
It will leave you with a longing desire to be with her every day
And with a ferocious fire of desire burning passionately through your veins.
You won't be able to contain yourself, you'll want to let her know how you feel;
Telling her and always showing her how she's the center of your world.
By doing so, may the love of your life never leave you empty-handed;
Giving a reason to always hold on, no matter what the circumstances.
Never let your romance die, keep it alive, no matter what the cost.
For it is better to have loved and lost than to never have loved at all.

Now I, my friend, am a romantic, and a hopeful one at that.
For my romance is not hopeless, it has faith, love, and tact.
I have always been the kind who always wears his heart on his sleeve;
My heart is marked with deep cuts and scars defending my love of she.

September 2, 2013

Souldier

Born into life and left for dead;
Original sin had become my bed.

Beaten down, lonely, confused;
Crawling through life - I was always used.

Then one day a hand appeared;
A hand filled with love - it brought me to tears.

Christ's hand it was, offering to help;
Reaching out I took it, it was then that I felt...

Love, Joy, Friendship, and Peace;
Resurrecting my soul - never to cease.

Kneeling before my God and His Son;
With Spirit inside me - all three into one.

Blessed by my God, He equips me for battle;
It's the armor of God - that which I've saddled.

I am a soldier of God - now hear my cry;
"For I am the Battle-Worthy Bringer of Light!"

"I declare war on my sins and demons alike;
Even on Satan and principalities of no light!"

In the beginning it seemed God is No Where;
Truth opened my eyes - God is NoW here.

Luke = "Bringer of Light"
Harvey = "Battle-Worthy"

November 12, 2009

Shattered to Live Again

My mind is shattered, my heart is numb;
Breaking down, I now succumb.

Feeling weak and short of breath;
This is my time, I stare down death.

No more will I hide, no more will I fall.
I have taken a side, I have heard the call.

No more will I sit. No more will I “can’t”.
I have not quit. I have taken a stand.

My time is here. My time is now.
My prayer He hears; my prayer is how.

My body may break. My soul may ache.
I follow my lead, yet making mistakes.

Where do I go? What’s there to do?
Don’t care 'bout nothing, 'cept only You.

November 6, 2009

The Birth of an Idea

It begins with a single Thought, born of a Dream, perched on a precipice of the mind. A Thought of courage, of hope, of love daring to one day form into an Idea. A creation of wonder and majesty cloaked in a poetic nuance amid the surrounding chaos of uncollected dreams.

Like a flower the Thought forms and grows waiting to bloom into an Idea. Chaos carved out of old rhetoric threatens the very existence of the

Thought. But it is through this chaos, through the fires of turmoil, the formed Thought begins to transform. The Dream that became a Thought has now become an Idea.

Love and passion collide creating the catalyst to form the voice of the Idea. Dying to be heard it cries out but only a whimper. Waiting for a response nothing happens. Its voice too muffled by the pangs of the Outside; only heard by its own echoes off the walls of empty promises waiting to be fulfilled.

But the Idea is structured with persistence, resolve, and perseverance. Not willing to allow its voice die quietly into the good night cries out with purpose encapsulated with hope, faith, and conviction. The voice of the Idea breaks through the paper walls penetrating into the canyons and precipices of other minds.

It ends with a new single Thought perched on the precipice of another mind. It dares to one day form into a vocal Idea, like that of its ancestor with a voice that would one day break through the chaos to be heard. Heard so that one day it would bring forth dreams over nightmares and turn thoughts into change.

January 1, 2023

Bitten - But Not Shy

I'm caught in this web of who I should and shouldn't be,
Where lines are blurred between truth and deceit.

A little distraction is what I thought I needed.
The kiss of your lips made me so heated.

I was broken inside. I thought you could save me.
Instead I gave in to your rejection and trickery.

But again I was wrong – I meant nothing to you.
You forgot me as fast as the moment I met you.

I'm focused now, fastened in, buckled up.
Watch out for me now so back the fuck up!

The saying goes “Once Bitten, Twice Shy”,
But I’ve been bitten before and can tell you
that’s a lie!

I embrace these bites I’ve been given and wear
them as scars
To remember you by and how you left your
mark.

I can never forget what happened on that night,
Etched vividly in living color, screw the black
and white.

Now I turn my eyes to what really matters most:
Sure as hell ain't you, that's no joke.

June 4, 2013

Someday

Someday I'll be where I want to be
Without weighted shoulders or a glass half-empty.
Taking in a deep full breath,
Finding new ways to unwind and relax.

Someday I will live my life,
Undictated, living each day just the way I like.
Where I won't be stuck in a rut
Working 7 to 7 just to get my cut.

But what if Someday never comes?
Will I regret it and fail to see the sun?
Should I just hold my breath,
Or let it all out risking to blow out the match?

Someday I will cash in all my chips
For the endless blessings I've been promised.
Throwing back what life's dished out
And not be tempted to throw in the towel.

But what if that day finally comes
And I live my life full in the sun?
Finally able to take a breath
And learn to be without regret.

January 31, 2023

Reflections of the Deep

I write this not just for fun, you see,
But may it be an inspiration for you from me.

You may be lost, lonely, scared, or confused;
Wondering where to go or what you should do.

Know that I have been there before, my friend.
Yes, it can be trying and taxing and can be
enough to send you to the end.

We live in a ripple-effect world where actions
clash with decisions.
When you are tired, sometimes it's best to be
still to avoid a collision.

Be true to the four that ultimately matter the
most;
Yourself with The Father, The Son, and The
Holy Ghost.

Be slow to anger and slow to react in your own
defense;
Lest then you show foolishness along with your
ignorance.

Be quick to pick up a brother or guide a lost
sister;
It reflects upon your Father and shows building
relationships is the answer.

Take heed, for I say these words are not just
mine,
But they are words of our Father, for with Him
we all shine.

June 25, 2013

Turtle Doves

When the weight of the world is crushing you down before you're outta bed.
And tears flavor your morning coffee as the raincloud's over your head.
Last night's dreams are like a retreat from this nightmare you're living in.
Where magic is real and there's something you feel to make life worth it all again.

When your best friend asks how you're doing and reply with just an "OK";
But all you want to do is drop the mask 'cause inside you're starting to decay.

A wink and a nod with nerves shot to hell,
charading a smile to hide your frown.
But inside you're screamin', barely breathin',
feelin' like you're about to drown.

Think all your thoughts, feel all your feelings,
but baby don't forget;
You are special and you are loved and you can
move mountains without fret.
The weight of the world is on your shoulders
when you should be soaring above;
Because you are not alone when you are one in a
pair of turtle doves.

Looking back on the choices in your life like a
"Choose Your Own Adventure" book;
You start to question what you've done and
every choice you made or never took.
Dreaming of going back in time, wishing you
could take a different path;
Wondering if it would lead you to salvation or
bring you to where you're at.

When your emotions are knotted and tangled
and all you want is to unwind;
But your body keeps moving and your mind's
always running on Play, Fast-Forward, or
Rewind.

Reliving the past and wondering if you are
where you're supposed to be;
The past is familiar. Right now is forever. The
future is a mystery.

So think all your thoughts, feel all your feelings,
but baby don't forget;
You are special. You are loved. You bring me to
life with a single breath.
The weight of the world is on your shoulders
when you should be soaring above;
Because you are not alone when you are one in a
pair of turtle doves.

When you fight so hard just to stay caught up,
each day feels like a damn year;
It's like trying to outrun your own reflection that
you see shown in the mirror.
Your voice has changed and there's a new
rhythm beating to the song playing in your heart;
Your new language is lyrics, for anyone who
listens they will understand your heart.

So when the weight of the world is on your
shoulders when you should be soaring above;
Just remember you are not alone when you are
one in a pair of turtle doves.

February 1, 2023

www.ingramcontent.com/pod-product-compliance
Lightning Source LLC
Chambersburg PA
CBHW051743130826
49812CB00033B/976
* 9 7 8 9 3 5 7 4 4 2 1 7 6 *